featherpaths

featherpaths

clyde holmes

ISBN: 0-86381-886-2

Cover design and inside illustrations: Kim Atkinson

Published with the financial support of the Welsh Books Council

First published in 2004 by
Gwasg Carreg Gwalch, 12 Iard yr Orsaf, Llanrwst,
Wales LL26 OEH
Tel: 01492 642031   Fax: 01492 641502
e-mail: books@carreg-gwalch.co.uk   website: www.carreg-gwalch.co.uk

Acknowledgements

Acknowledgements are due to the editors of the following in which some of these poems have appeared:

Anglo-Welsh Review, Aquarius, Cyphers, Honest Ulsterman, London Magazine, New Welsh Review, Poetry Wales

Anthologies: *Speak to the Hills*, Hamish Brown and Martin Berry eds., Aberdeen University Press; *Birdsong*, Seren

Contents

Foreword

I was born in London and moved to northern Wales in 1970 to live, write and paint at a remote farmhouse, Cwm Hesgin, in the uplands of Snowdonia near Bala.

My poetry is a celebratory act springing out of my concern for the wilder aspects of nature. The land where I live is wild, wet and full of life. It is a sanctuary for rare birds of prey, plants and insects. For the past few years this area has been a Site of Special Scientific Interest (SSI), protected by the Countryside Council of Wales.

My approach to writing is succinctly expressed by Jonathan Bate in his book *Song of the Earth*:

'To be a nature poet (or more aptly an eco-poet) you have to be essentially a "dweller" or "inmate" who feels with nature, developing an attunement to the spirit of the place over many years.'

'What would the world be once bereft
Of wet and wildness? Let them be left,
O let them be left, wildness and wet;
Long live the weeds and the wilderness yet.'
                    Gerard Manley Hopkins, *Inversnaid*

Clyde Holmes, 2004

Introduction

This is a beautiful collection of 48 quiet, intensely imagined poems. Each focuses on a bird captured within a moment in time. The poems are spare, stripped of extraneous ornamentation with a kind of weightlessness that reflects their subject matter. The absence of intricate verbal and intellectual games is both a pleasure and a gift communicating the poet's own ability to concentrate on essentials and evoking an equivalent responsiveness in the reader.

The assured control of word and tone in each poem makes the collection cohere very satisfyingly into a whole. The lack of a narrative development gives the reader freedom to dip amongst the poems at random.

As for the individual poems – I could select almost any of them for praise. The end of 'Hearing Ode' for example, shows the poet's superb control of closure, detailing a range of bird voices then closing on the gap in the chorus: 'what I still miss most/is the harrier over rushes,/that soundless waver.' The final stanza of 'Curlew' closes quite differently, demonstrating the precision and strangeness of an Old English riddle:

Combines sound and silence,
brushes air with soft vigour,
slides across sloe-blue hills –
vehicle of wind's roaring breath.

The central stanza of the very next poem, 'Curlews' Nest', itself matches 'the machine-gun rhythms' of an anxious parent faced with human intruders: 'incensed wing-flames,/an aerial attack/sputtering his aggression.' 'Skylark' summons up the rich compression of Emily Dickinson, each poised, weighed word, hanging, balanced on the page, like the bird that is its fragile subject. In 'Lapwing' the subject is again mirrored in this style, the sudden drop of the bird falling out of the sky reflected in the emphatic rhyme that (unusually) closes the verse: 'crash-landing his inborn skill./Icarus survives on a rush-thatched hill.' ·

The poet is not just good at attention to form or matching rhythm to subject matter. He is adept at the daring simile. I loved the stunning simile that closed 'Swallows' where the birds' rapidity removes them from the space and time of normality and creates artists of the onlooker, drawing together past and present as their quills sketch

on today's blank sheet
of air and water,
Leonardo's lightning hands.

The intense interpretative gaze of 'Magpie in Winter' relates subject to immediate context, the eye casting back and forth between mountain and bird, assessing and qualifying. In 'West Wings' both movement and sound of the roosting rooks become almost visible –

permanent silhouettes
(from conjurors' hats) bewilder space –
air brims with hoarse drawls.

– while 'Reflections on a Hen Harrier' mulls over the multiple significances of 'reflections' in the context of 'the long migration of light [and] . . . the sun's power.'

On the whole these poems stand as honed and intense meditations on the intensely inhabited world outside the human window. They are extremely accessible drawing very little on learned or abstruse learning. Yet they suggest a world of magic if the reader would only look more intensely. It is appropriate therefore that one of the only references to Classical mythology should be to the mythical poet who charmed the stones and trees: Orpheus. In 'Willow Warbler' the poet draws attention to the inhabitation of the ordinary by the fantastic declaring that 'year after year/Orpheus returns. In 'Severmore' another appears in the Spring-driven wagtail, desperately fighting his own reflection in the window:

The crazed feathery Narcissus
made drum skins
of our window-panes,
slapped out quavers
with beak and wings

but neither of these references are abstruse enough to put off the reader.

The final line of the final poem of the collection, 'Cwm Hesgin',
demonstrates yet again the poet's facility with endings: 'my door darkens
open'.

I loved these poems and read them with enormous pleasure. The
subject matter is uncontroversial and popular (without being populist).

Dr Jeni Williams

Redstart

I never knew how much
the bird was his name
until that summer he nested in
the drystone wall of my barn.

A rust-red dart
targeting foliage
a stone's throw
from his crack of shadow.

The low-flying messenger
posted himself into rock and tree,
shrugged off the open ground.
No time for higher pursuits –
sky the mirror of his absence.

Barn Owl

Cwm Hesgin

Shook himself
off the roof's shoulder
and seemed unaware
of me sitting there,
cup in hand, outside the farmhouse.

With a little help
from a gibbous moon
I saw him for the first time
not startled by light. He wafted
from pigsty to coalshed
then entered the sky-night
through an old windowframe.

He was lost from sight,
but I heard him
brush off star-flakes.

Eagle Owl

Cwm Hesgin
for Simon and Liz

Arrives in the back of a landrover,
scuffles from the tail-board
to our cradle, his make-shift perch
after the chainsaw's dust-showers.

His deep cidery eyes,
reflecting another autumn,
are targets for our destruction.
He blinks in the crystal-blue
afternoon, foretelling death
above our glaring mound.

His talons poised,
a last bid to wrench hearts
from forests' owl-light.

Owl

Sits alone
in the sycamore.
His moaning coos
waver through darkness.
Our window-glare
his night's oasis.

We move around
in the house, project
our brief shadows.
He echoes life's eclipses,
our pining for light.

Ring Ouzels

Flank the hill,
pied pipers at nightfall.
Clear notes ring out.

After brief stay
they carry luck away
from farms –

horseshoes on their breasts
brand darkness.

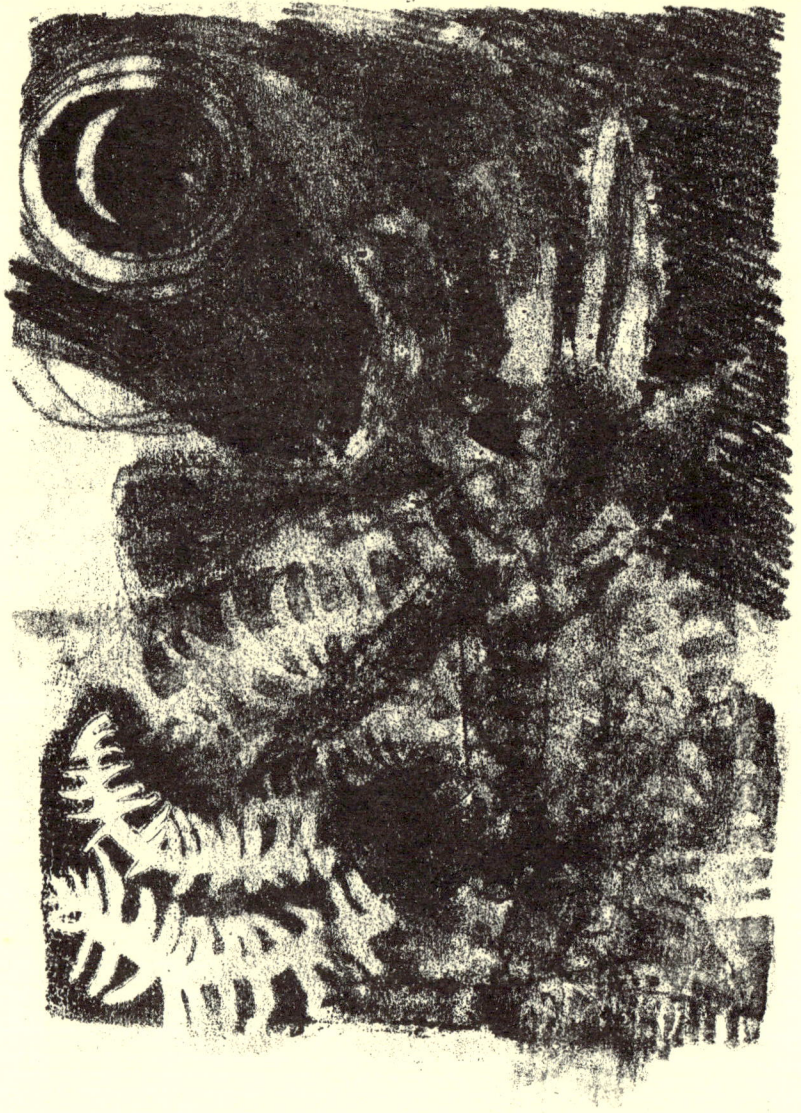

Nightjarred

On summer evenings
we crouched in bracken
breathless for his rattling tingle,

crashed through dense stillness
to unveil log-coloured plumage
matching his richly decayed notes.

Always deceived
by his ventriloquial expertise.
Once (between churrs) he startled us –

wings tilted upwards, handlebars
wheeling himself around
with pipistrelle outriders;

the volatile, puckish presence,
ghosting his voice,
left us in sound-shadow.

Hearing Ode

Cwm Hesgin

It was the hope-filled call
that first poured out
of my tiny Pandora's box.
The silent spring became
a strident recording of birdsong.

All day dawn chorused,
drew me to sightings
of skylark, curlew
and the cuckoo
I thought no longer flew here.
But what I still miss most
is the harrier over rushes,
that soundless waver.

Curlew

With boomerang-shaped wings
cuts sky,
skater set in motion
by a sheet of ice.

Alone with his own
weird bubbling whistle,
steers, bow-beaked,
past grazing cloud,
isolates day and land.

Combines sound and silence,
brushes air with soft vigour,
slides across sloe-blue hills –
vehicle of wind's roaring breath.

Curlews' Nest

Must be near the farmhouse.
For weeks now
he gasps with a wheezy scream.
Above my head, his curved bill
an ominous, sabred silhouette.

Incensed wing-flames.
An aerial attack
sputtering his aggression
in machine-gun rhythms.

When I step out
of his circled territory
his sound magically ceases.
I am stunned by silence –
freed from his anxiety.

Skylark

Resonant, air-thrilled ascent –

wings flicker,
hold stone-bird
until he plummets
into sky's shimmering depth –

leaves me an eavesdropper
straining after diminished song –
his harp's expanding circles.

Lapwing

Climbs towards sun,
frantically waves,
wings are wide sleeves.

In love with falling,
crash-landing his inborn skill.
Icarus survives on a rush-thatched hill.

Bryn Selwrn

for Annette et al

Its high, square walls cleave
space. Behind the house
flies' punctuation
is being erased
from a swallow-crazed sky.
A shed's pouched beam
the still centre
of their turning world.

Above the front garden
air is left alone
between the trees' canopy.
Inside space too is divided,
all revolving around
the big kitchen's cooker
before darting to our own nooks.
Each bedroom a nest
shaped by the body's language.

Chickens

Are senseless in the dark –

reborn every morning
with the cock's bugling.

Deep-pink glow of combs
sunrise their heads
sparring with shed's
rectangle of fresh light.

Inveterate scratchers –
claw-roots in soil.
All day beaks peg ground.

Fold themselves up
before night comes –

always ahead of the sun.

Swallows

Shoot past our windows,
their bodies cutting off light,
flashes in reverse.

They defy real time,
race through millennia,
their quills sketching

on today's blank sheet
of air and water,
Leonardo's lightning hands.

Swallow Haiku

Swallow-thoughts dissolve
boundary between my brain
and the deep blue dome.

Fieldfare

Scudding nebula of wings
scatters itself across the hillside,
leaf-flocks on bare boughs.

A Viking horde
pillages uplands –
returns to Scandinavia.

Magpie in Winter

The snow was almost gone,
most of it washed away by heavy rain,
gobbed into bulging watercourses;

it was leaving piebald rock
and sheep changed back
from sallow-grey to white again.

His plumage matched the mountain
as if snow, melting on his wing,
released him from frozen stillness.

Arctic Tern

Non-stop from pole to pole, never lags;
Columbus saw her through cloud-bergs
and thought he was close to land.

Sun seldom roosts beneath her horizon;
night-time melts on her wing-span,
a translucent astrolabe.

Seagulls

Above cliffs
clouds drift with them.

Sun, a dazzling brooch
on their staggering breasts.

Wings make shadows on them,
fly in waterfalls of light.

Bodies of sea
wings of sky.

Grouse

Suddenly the propeller-like whirr –
raucous chortle of startled grouse
beats itself out
(from a bunch of branches).

Just above heather
a long stiff-winged glide
until lost from sight.

After the brief disturbance,
silence, space and colour
return to the bird.

Peacocks

Roam the gardens
in their head-high vegetation,
aloof survivors of a lost paradise.
Now they proclaim mating time,

transplant air's burgeoning scene
to banks of the Hydaspes –
echo Alexander's battle
cries at his world's end.

West Wings

Hafod y Calch, for Steve & Jenny

In the window-pane
old bullet holes punctuate the view,
pauses between shots' stampeding.

Outside wings arch
with ominous lassitude,
carry rooks towards their roost.

Sun's lingering glow
turns leafless crowns to charcoal,
watch-towers litter branches;

permanent silhouettes
(from conjurors' hats) bewilder space –
air brims with hoarse drawls.

Crow Haiku

One crow flying low
over the sun-flushed heather
with his shadow mate.

Choughs

Ronda Gorge, Andalucia

Back home we still see them.
Their black pages
flipping in wind,
shifting our thoughts.

From the New Bridge
we'd watched them threading
through arches, knew
cracks from mere shadow.

Your pupils snatched
their flight in miniatures.
Looking down
they plumbed our abyss.

Griffon Vultures

for Martin, Annie, John & Viv

Sierra de Cazorla, Spain

We drive
to the sierra's crest
and reach their level.

Distant aerial carousels
become giant outstretched hands
stroking the sky's back.

Life for them a perpetual glide.
No need for wing-beats
they ride on departed souls.

Storks

Periscopes watching us
from wicker cauldrons,
guarding their future
walled-in by shell.

Beyond ramparts
wind furrows sand and cloud.
Storks sweep above
white-housed hills.

Palm-fronds mirror
the slow bounce of wings.

Cattle Egret

near Tarifa

The village's white-walled glare
rings the hilltop;
they breed fighting bulls here.

In the field an egret flutters
his wing-cape before a bullock
who knows no other matador.

Kite

Sabhanayaka Temple, Chidambaram

Krishna is everywhere
lording it over gopuras.
Even the initial shared
is no coincidence.

They are one being
of course, aspects of each other.
He prefers bathing
in air, picks off frogs at will;

leaves stench of the temple's
tank to his worshippers,
for their immersion in rituals.

Tirthas

Paddy bird, Tamil Nadu

I was drawn to this bird
all over Tamil Nadu.
On fetid patches of bank
the dull, mud-brown bystander

waited for its moment
to cross rivers.
Then a feathery flash,
an unsheathing of translucent,

white wings, briefly fanning
a burnt out space.
The Magician
nowhere to be seen.

Note:
Holy places in India are called tirthas. It means, in Sanskrit, crossing place of a river. But also tirtha means crossing place between the human world and the divine.

Herons

In bustle of tree-tops
the heron thrives with others,
does not collide with them
or, in their tracks, blunder.

In air suspends himself,
vaults sky with wings
that droop and yield to absence.

Skulks alone in soggy texture
by mountain tarns, stands motionless
taking aim, an archer,
fishes and frogs for targets.

Immutable and bone-thin,
space immense about him.

Red Kites

Gigrin Farm breeding site

We watched them for an hour
cornering the beef market
amongst bustling corvines
moving our heads in unison
behind the hide's glass.

In a cloud-filled aquarium
it was all down
to a flick of the tail-fin.
Their forked third wing tuned them
in to a flight-life of mugging.

Merlins' Nest

Llyn Hesgin

The tarnside rowan, a month-old home.
Four chocolate-tinged worlds,
gift-wrapped in wool, held
in a shaky blend of leaves, water and wind.

We goose-step the heather.
Carry out the raid.
Eggs measured and weighed
then her turn, headfirst into a bag.

A few seconds wing-stillness.
Your palm an altar
for the offering – the flaw
back to sun-eyed cumulus.

Mallards

Tail-backs of ripples
fuse – the mallard and his mate
wing-scatter water.

Upland Nativity

It's Christmas day.
Sheep and shepherd have gone.
Sky a Madonna-blue

by the frozen tarn, no offerings
of voles and pipits.
Here, on a heather-clad spur,

the deserted merlin's nest
a cradle in the rowan,
one star hinting at its presence.

Buzzard

Orbits the hill.
Stilled wings tremble,
tip him to another ridge;

leads me into his space –
earth circles sun, preys
upon it for life.

Kestrel

He's not a bird
that distracts me.
Throughout the day

he's there in ether
fluttering at half-mast,
but clear of toil and distress.

Often, while I'm digging,
I see him stoop below the ridge,
a samara burying itself in flesh.

 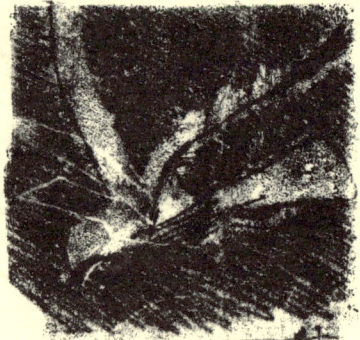

 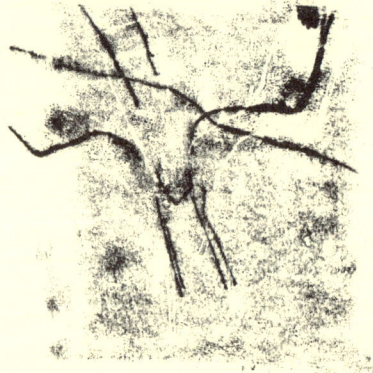

Hen Harriers

I

Delivered himself regularly
to the valley,
carried news of nothing
but his presence.

Daily I followed his spread
of wings as he read
the ground just beneath him,
finely tuned to each tussock.

Screens of flickering
light and shade showed him
real images of flesh and blood.

II

On a remote tarn
only his reflection
is wind-surfing:
water his ruffled plumage.
He keels over, his wing-
waves conjured from the surface.

He shins up air,
slides down again
to his heather-bound mate;
she's fallen for his stunts
and the vigour
of his aerial limping.
A shot here would
shatter the sky dance.
For a few months
the blanket bog has an albatross.

III

We watched him spellbound.
Had he wished for a small portion
of cloud-shadow to tip,
like arrows, his snow-white wings,

so that he too could be
atoned with wind, casting himself
over mountains, never missing
the quiver of his soft targets?

Or had his pledge been broken
and he condemned to a limbo
close to land, always
mobbed by his own black primaries?

Reflections on a Hen Harrier

His white wings flashed –
tilted just above ground to meet
the long migration of light.

Made me think
of my first experiment
in open air, lens hovering

until grass smouldered
preying on the sun's power.

Willow Warbler

Year after year
Orpheus returns
to his sky's underworld.

The cool green cave
echoes again
with spring's song

pouring from buds' throats –
each dribbling stream of notes
deepens his shade.

Dipper

Flows on air
with his reach of river;
disappears, doubles back
in narrow meanders.

Perches on rock;
a buoy bobbing
in and out of swift water
jellying round him.

Watersmith
forging his song
from molten ripples.

Cuckoo

Echoes himself –

sounding out
his isolation
with tuneful hiccuping.

Patrols for pipits.
Nests bombed by eggs –

brittle explosions
of his own gawky flesh.

Pigeons

Clatter from woods,
shrug off bluebells'
fallen patch of sky,

escape
their earthly reflection –
wings forever applauding themselves.

Severmore

All through April
our house was under siege.
You'd think he'd overflown
his watery element,
so desperate was he to drown
in his own reflection.

The crazed feathery Narcissus
made drum-skins
of our window panes,
slapped out quavers
with beak and wings.

Our room-deep mirror
beyond the wagtail's glass war.

Great Spotted Woodpecker

Cwm Hesgin, March '03

Early morning holds its breath.
From today we're at war.
I turn off the radio. Hear
The woodpecker's shudder.

Budgerigar Blues

His sun-shocked plumage came
from the austral side of the globe.
It was mid-winter in north Wales.
Colours here his faded echoes
from hills' yellowy-green breasts
and died-back rush crests.

He'd flashed through the door's slit.
No perching on fencelines,
too much like cages.
Our kids stood aghast,
followed the ridge's flight pattern
swooping to his extinction.

Llyn Hesgin

Tufted duck carving
out sky as they glide through tarn's
mountain reflection.

Cwm Hesgin

Wedged in the top of a hill
I am a house full of change,
daily living in claustral embrace
is never the same.

I have three names
sunrise, sunset and midday.
Between many-eyed cloud sun squirms,
shadow sweeps uphill then returns.

Prolonged gloom in my room
interrupted only by swallows
blinking my small windows.

I follow a gull within my eye
beyond the haloed mountain –
my door darkens open.

Also by Clyde Holmes:
In Season (Embers Press, 1988)
Skywalls (Gwasg Carreg Gwalch, 1998)